# My Easter Book
## In My Own Words
## All About Me

*Written by Faye Deaton Brophy and Sharon Gordon*
*Illustrated by Faye Deaton Brophy*

Tell your story!
Just fill in the blanks using words,
pictures, or photos.

This book belongs to _____.
This book was given by _____.
Date _____

## Troll Associates

**It's Easter —** one of my favorite holidays! To me, Easter is a very special day because _____ _____. The first thing I do when I wake up on Easter morning is _____ _____. Then my family and I like to _____ _____ and _____.

2

(Use this space to draw a picture or paste in a photo.)

Here is a picture of something that always makes me glad it's Easter.

# My Easter Basket

I would like to find these things in my Easter
basket: _____
_____. I would really be surprised if I
found _____ in my basket this
year. My Easter basket might be decorated with
_____ and _____.
My favorite Easter candy is_____
and _____
and _____.

Here is a picture of my
Easter basket.

# Easter Eggs

Coloring Easter eggs is so much fun. The most eggs I ever colored by myself was _____. This is a picture of an Easter egg I decorated.

Here are lots of ideas for making your Easter eggs extra special. Look around your house. You'll find many things to use for your decorations. Have fun!

## What you need:

Scissors, glue, crayons, nontoxic markers, construction paper, yarn, pipe cleaners, scraps of fabric, straws, dried flowers, bottle caps, pompons.

## What you do:

1 Dye and dry your eggs.

2 Choose a design you like or make up one of your own.

3 Legs, wings, wheels, collars, and hats can be cut from construction paper. Glue them into place. Use pompons for hair, noses, tails. Pipe cleaners can be used for legs, tails, and antennas. Bits of fabric are good for clothing and hats. Use your markers to write messages, to add fancy decorations, or to fill in the details.

# My Easter Story

I enjoy hearing the story of how the Easter Bunny delivers his colorful eggs. But I think it would be funny if one year, something silly like this happened on Easter:

The silliest thing happened on Easter morning. I awoke at _____ o'clock when I heard a loud _____ outside my window. I peeked through the curtains and saw the Easter Bunny dressed like _____! He was wearing _____ and _____ _____, with _____ on his head. To my surprise, the Easter Bunny carried his eggs in a _____ instead of a basket. Then, he sat down under a tree and _____ the eggs instead of hiding them. Afterward, he hopped away and began singing _____. I hope the Easter Bunny isn't acting so _____ _____ next year!

It would be fun to go on an Easter-egg hunt. I think _____ _____ would be the perfect place to have an egg hunt. I might find eggs hidden _____ and _____. This is one place I would *not* want to find an egg hidden: _____! It would be funny if my friend _____ found _____ _____ instead of an egg. This is something funny that might happen during an Easter-egg hunt: _____ _____ _____.

Here is a picture of me looking for Easter eggs.

# Easter-Egg Maze

Let's go on an Easter-egg hunt. Can you find your way through the eggs to the bunny? How many eggs can you find along the way?

END

(Answers on page 13.)

START

# My Easter-Egg Holders

## What you need:

Construction paper

Pencil

Scissors

Crayons or markers

Tape

## What you do:

1 Cut strips of construction paper of the size shown on the next page. Decorate them with crayons or markers. Tape ends together to form a circle.

2 Trace or draw the animals shown—or make up some of your own! Color them. Tape each animal to the back of a holder.

3 Place colored egg in holder.

This is a picture of my egg holders.

12

Decorate your egg holders
any way you like. Here are
some ideas.

LOVE YOU

*Answer to maze from page 11:*
There are 30 eggs in all.

13

# Fun Easter Hats

Everyone needs a special hat to wear in the Easter parade!

**To make a top hat, you will need:**

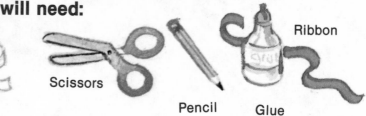

Cardboard

Tape

Scissors

Pencil

Glue

Ribbon

## What you do:

1  Roll the cardboard into a cylinder to fit your head. Tape the ends together. At the top and bottom of the cylinder cut flaps all around the hat that are 2 inches deep.

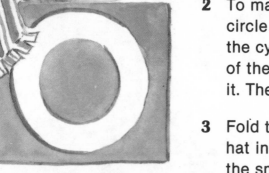

2  To make a brim, cut a large circle out of cardboard. Place the cylinder in the center of the circle and trace around it. Then cut out the inner circle.

3  Fold the flaps at the top of your hat inward and glue or tape the smaller circle to the flaps.

4  Turn the flaps at the bottom of the hat outward. Push the brim over the hat until it rests on the flaps. Glue brim to flaps. Now decorate your top hat with ribbon or anything else you like.

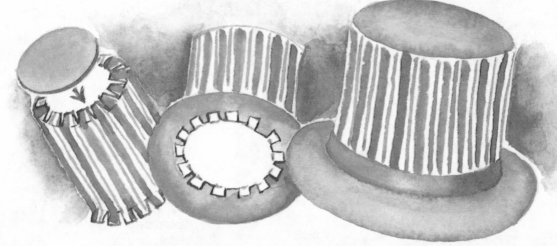

# To make an Easter bonnet, you will need:

Scissors

Paper or straw flowers

Paper plate

Tape or glue

Cardboard

Pencil

Ribbon

Lace

## What you do:

1 Bend cardboard into a semicircle to fit your head. Cut flaps at the back of the bonnet that are 2 inches deep.

2 From another piece of cardboard, cut out a shape to fit the back of the bonnet. Turn flaps inward and glue the back of the bonnet to them.

3 Punch a hole on each side of the bonnet. Knot 2 lengths of ribbon to the bonnet for ties. Now decorate your hat!

## Paper-Plate Bonnet

1 Center a length of ribbon onto plate and attach with glue or tape.

2 Glue straw or paper flowers to paper plate.

Now you're ready for the Easter parade.

15

# My Easter Parade

I would like to be in charge of planning an Easter parade for my town. It would start _____ and then go down these streets: _____ _____. I would want the streets to be decorated with _____ and _____ _____. I would ask these people to be in the parade: _____.

I would ask this famous person to be in it, too: _____
_____. There would be music at the parade. The band would play these songs: _____
_____. My friends _____ and
_____ would serve snacks like _____
_____, _____, and _____.

We would wear the Easter hats we made. Here is a picture of me at the Easter parade.

# Spring

I love Easter because it means that spring is in the air! The first flowers I see in the spring are _____ and _____. My favorite Easter flower is _____. If I had a garden, these are some other flowers I would plant: _____.

Spring is also a time when you see lots of baby animals. Once I saw a baby _____ at _____.
Someday I would love to see a baby _____.
I hope I never see a baby _____!
If I was given three baby bunnies for Easter, I would name them _____,
_____, and _____
_____. I would feed them
_____ and teach
them _____. This is
where they would sleep: _____
_____.

# Jellybean and Candy-Chick Cake

One of the reasons I love jellybeans is because they are so colorful. I think it would be fun to decorate a cake with jellybeans! First, I would start with my favorite: _____ _____ cake with _____ icing. Then I would add designs with lots of jellybeans. These are the colors I would use: _____.

Here is a picture of my jellybean cake.

Candy chicks could be put in the center, sitting on a nest of shredded coconut. (Color the coconut green with food coloring before using.)

# Bunny Bread

Here's something for Easter dinner that looks pretty and tastes good, too.

## What you need:

Butter

Cookie sheet

2 Cans refrigerator biscuits or cinnamon rolls (20 biscuits needed)

## What you do:

1   Grease cookie sheet with butter.

2   Open cans. Preheat oven according to directions on package. (Ask a grownup to help you with the oven.)

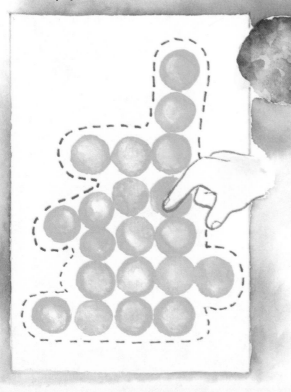

3   Place rolls on cookie sheet as shown. Press gently to close spaces between rolls.

4   Decorate with cherries or raisins and bake as directed on package. After Bunny Bread is cooked, add icing, if cinnamon rolls have been used.

21

# My Easter Clay

## What you need:

1 Cup flour    ¼ Cup salt    ⅓ Cup water    Mixing bowl    Paints    Clear nail polish

Paintbrush    Spoon    Plastic bag

## What you do:

1  Put your flour, salt, and water in a bowl.

2  Mix well, pressing with your fingers to get out any lumps. If clay feels dry, add a few drops of water. If it feels too mushy, add a bit of flour.

3  Store the clay in a plastic bag in the refrigerator.

4  Let your figures dry at room temperature or bake at 350 degrees for ½ to 1 hour.

**5** Clay can be braided, twisted, or rolled out for use with cookie cutters. Use a garlic press or sieve to make tiny strands of hair for your figurines. You might like to color your finished characters with paints. Then paint them with clear nail polish to give them a nice shine.

Here are some examples of what you can make for Easter.

I think there should be a special cookie shaped like the Easter Bunny. This is the flavor I would want it to be: _____ _____. Then, for decoration, I would make his eyes out of _____, his nose out of _____ _____, and his ears out of _____. For a fluffy little tail, I would use _____. What a delicious cookie!

## Bunny Cookies!

### What you need:

1 Cup softened butter

½ Cup sugar

2½ Cups flour

½ Teaspoon almond extract

Bunny-shaped cookie cutter

Round cookie cutter

*Optional:* Sprinkles, cherries, raisins, coconut

## What you do:

**1** With a large spoon, blend butter and sugar in a bowl. Mix well.

**2** Stir in the flour and almond extract.

**3** Shape dough into small balls; then flatten them out to about ¼ inch thick. Using bunny-shaped cookie cutter, cut out bunnies.

**4** *To make bunny head:* use round cookie cutter. Cut out two circles. Cut one circle in half for ears and press them to top of head.

**5** Decorate bunnies with sprinkles, coconut, cherries, and raisins.

**6** Place cookies on greased cookie sheet and chill in refrigerator for ½ hour.

**7** With a grownup's help, heat oven to 300 degrees.

**8** Bake cookies for 30 minutes. Do not brown.

25

# My Easter Cards

I would like to make an Easter card and send it to _____ _____. There would be a picture of _____ _____ on the cover, with the message "_____ _____" on the inside. Here is how it would look.

Easter cards are fun and easy to make. Here's how.

**What you need:**

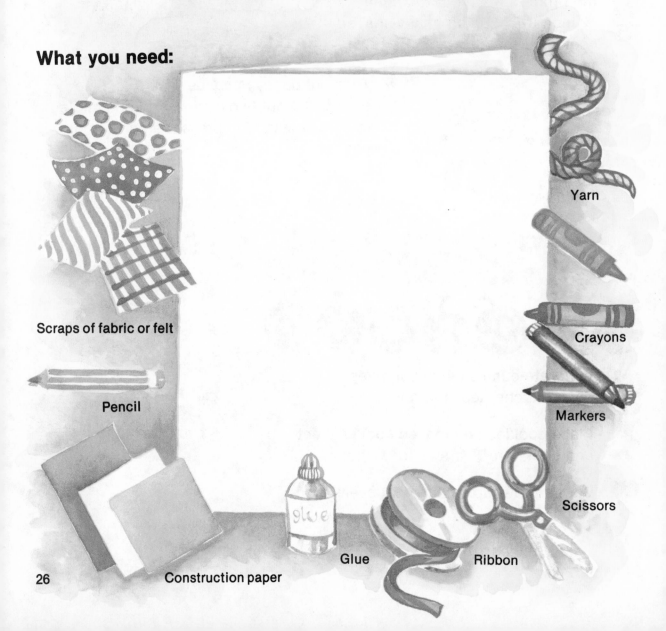

Scraps of fabric or felt

Pencil

Construction paper

Glue

Ribbon

Yarn

Crayons

Markers

Scissors

## What you do:

**1** Fold a sheet of construction paper in half to make the card.

**2** Plan your design. Here are some examples. Designs can be cut from fabric, ribbon, or yarn and glued into place.

**3** Use crayons or markers to draw designs, to fill in details, and to write your Easter message.

HAPPY EASTER

**4** By putting together these easy basic shapes, you can draw bunnies and chicks.

27

# The Easter Bunny's House

It's fun to imagine the Easter Bunny's house. I think it would
be made of _____ and would be
shaped like _____. It would be painted
these colors: _____.
This is how I colored the Easter Bunny's house.

If I went to visit the Easter Bunny, he would ask me to come in and eat some _____ and _____ _____. Then he would take me to meet his famous neighbors: _____ and _____. Before I left, the Easter Bunny would give me _____ _____ as a present. Here is a picture of me and the Easter Bunny in front of his house.

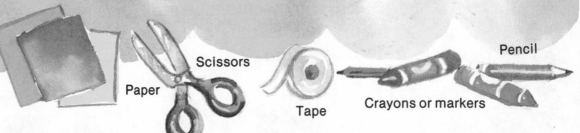

# My Easter Garlands

## What you need:

Paper

Scissors

Tape

Crayons or markers

Pencil

## What you do:

1 Cut strips of paper that are 3½ inches tall by 11 inches wide.

2 Fold strip of paper in half. Fold it in half again...and then again. It will look like this.

3 Press paper together and draw one of the designs shown on the next page on top of the paper.

4 Hold folded paper together and cut out the design you've drawn. Open carefully. Using crayons or markers, color your garlands, if you like. To make longer garlands, repeat and tape together.

After making my Easter garlands, I would like to hang them _____ and _____. I would also like to decorate a present for _____ _____ with my garlands.

This giant Easter egg was colored by a
famous artist—me!